Tiny House

*The Definitive Build Manual of a
Tiny Home Specializing in Sustainable
Tiny House Living*

Austin Knight

© Copyright 2017 by Austin Knight - All rights reserved.

The follow eBook is reproduced below with the goal of providing information that is as accurate and reliable as possible. Regardless, purchasing this eBook can be seen as consent to the fact that both the publisher and the author of this book are in no way experts on the topics discussed within and that any recommendations or suggestions that are made herein are for entertainment purposes only. Professionals should be consulted as needed prior to undertaking any of the action endorsed herein.

This declaration is deemed fair and valid by both the American Bar Association and the Committee of Publishers Association and is legally binding throughout the United States.

Furthermore, the transmission, duplication or reproduction of any of the following work including specific information will be considered an illegal act irrespective of if it is done electronically or in print. This extends to creating a secondary or tertiary copy of the work or a recorded copy and is only allowed with express written consent from the Publisher. All additional right reserved.

The information in the following pages is broadly considered to be a truthful and accurate account of facts and as such any inattention, use or misuse of the information in question by the reader will render any resulting actions solely under their purview. There are no scenarios in which the publisher or the original author of this work can be in any fashion deemed liable for any hardship or damages that may befall them after undertaking information described herein.

Additionally, the information in the following pages is intended only for informational purposes and should thus be thought of as universal. As befitting its nature, it is presented without assurance regarding its prolonged validity or interim quality. Trademarks that are mentioned are done without written consent and can in no way be considered an endorsement from the trademark holder.

Table of Contents

Introduction 5

Chapter 1: The Tiny House Lifestyle 7

Chapter 2: A Movement Toward Tiny Home Living 9

Chapter 3: The Eco-Friendly Benefits 15

Chapter 4: Smart Storage 24

Chapter 5: How To Build a Tiny House Following The Building Stages 36

Chapter 6: Design Dynamics and Building Plans 43

Chapter 7: Quotes for a New Home Build 53

Chapter 8: Success Stories 62

Conclusion 71

Introduction

Thank you for taking the time to download *Tiny House!*

As time goes by we have found ourselves trying to build a home to be new/different and inventive. By building a tiny house you will find this to be the perfect way to get your innovative eco-friendly home. You can have a smaller home, if you read on further to see what type of things are involved in doing so.

As you read into the depths of this book you will discover how and what is required to build a tiny house, but the information is not just simple explanations, you will read the vocabulary of those in the building industry. You will be told different key things that carpenters do in order to build a home and you will be able implement some of these steps in order to save money on your build.

This tiny house book is a complete guide on how to get stated with you're build. It gives you the ability to do a rough quote for yourself, if you are only contemplating building one. You will learn a great deal of innovative ways to save space and how to implement the space saving techniques.

The guide also offers a few floor plan examples in order to encourage and inspire the reader. It is a guide on how to build a tiny house with advice on every single building stage. It addresses the common misconceptions about the tiny home movement and why you would benefit from owning one of these spectacular homes.

Tiny houses have become more and more popular in recent years and with the housing market as is and the unavailability of cheap property. A tiny house is a spectacular way to reduce the things that you don't need in your life, to allow for more time for your dreams. This book is a guide to achieve that dream. Whether you want a movable home, a permanent residence, a guesthouse, or an off-grid home, this book will guide through every step of the process.

At the completion of this book you will have a good understanding of what a tiny house is and how to build one. By the end, you should be able to plan the entirety of the process of building your dream Tiny House.

Once again, thanks for downloading this book, I hope you find it to be helpful!

Chapter 1: The Tiny House Lifestyle

The life in a tiny home is one of the adventurer, you will love the eco-friendly life style as it gives you self-sustainability if you want it. You can make your home self-sustainable to allow you to travel and not have the constant high living expenses whilst your away.

Imagine the potential of just leaving your home whilst you travel to Europe for 6 months and you only have to pay the costs of the land rather than every other bill under the sun.

This allows you to enjoy those new experiences more because you're not stressing about your bills at home. I know for a fact that when I am travelling the world I don't want to worry about my bills and money because that reduces the amount of enjoyment I have meeting new people and doing adventurous activities.

Once you own a tiny home you can even travel with the home if that's your desire. One particular style of home is a portable home. This involves building and designing a home with solid bearers and joists as the sub floor to allow it to be placed on a large flat trailer. The portable Tiny House is smaller than the secured Tiny Home but can be designed in a way that it is ideal for a couple whilst travelling.

But the second style of a tiny home is a secured home, this is just like building a normal home but a lot smaller to reduce the costs of everything. You will find that this way of living is the new way of saving money and getting ahead if your behind. Even though your home may be ¼ of the size it can still be a spectacular home because you have the opportunity to build and design it yourself. Building a fixed or portable tiny home can be extremely fun because you get to use your creative mindset and design all sorts furnishings that will be space saving.

Living in a tiny home is a completely new feeling that you would not be used to. To give you an idea of how it would feel for those that are new to this concept, imagine living in your master bedroom and adding everything you need within it. You get this feeling of being enclosed in a tight place but it gives you a great satisfaction of organization and comfort. Even though you have a smaller room due to the number of furnishings, there are countless ways to space save in order to make you feel like you're just living in a normal master bedroom. Your master bedroom gives you that feeling of being home and able to relax and so will your tiny house if furnished and designed correctly.

Chapter 2: A Movement Toward Tiny Home Living

Many Americans used to pass down the family estate from generation to generation, but the times are a changing! The average span a person stays in their home is approximately 5 years—barely long enough to decorate and plant a yard. About the time homeowners have settled, career demands uproot them, and they must go through the hassle of putting their home up for sale, finding another home in a new location, and painstakingly moving all their belongings to another location. Our society has become a constant flux of migration from city to city, and the expenses are astronomical.

Over 70% of Americans are living from paycheck to paycheck, fighting long-standing debt that offers them no light at the end of the tunnel. One of the primary expenditures almost every adult has is a hefty mortgage. Just about the time homeowners begin to build a bit of equity in their homes, the next move happens, and they lose their investment in moving costs and Real estate fees. In the past, there has been little hope for financial freedom for most middle-class Americans. However, there's a movement underway that promises to lift the financially oppressed and encourage the free-spirited adventurers, and it's called "Tiny Homes."

Tiny Homes are offering people an option and an alternative lifestyle, with their hassle-free maintenance and self-sustaining designs. You would think that Tiny Homes would appeal to the young more, with their hearts full of adventure and their bank accounts emptied by the rising costs of education. While many young people do opt to live in Tiny Homes, almost 40% of today's owners are over 50 years old. Their need to downsize and simplify their lives has made the Tiny Home quite attractive.

With approximately 15 years of salaries devoted to covering a mortgage that is rarely paid in full and about a third to one-half of one's income going to pay for a mortgage, home maintenance, and comfort costs, it's no wonder Tiny Homes have become all the rage. Sixty-eight percent of those living in Tiny Homes have no mortgage at all, and aside from that, their savings reflect the significantly lowered living expenses with 55% of Tiny Home dwellers stockpiling much more money than the average American.

Take Back Your Life with a Tiny Home

In some ways, the movement of living in a Tiny Home began because people just wanted to take back their lives. The debt was controlling their lives, and the lack of mobility was hindering the dreams of many whose desires were to have the freedom and financial stability to enjoy travel and adventure. Instead of being committed to a goal of exploring new places and meeting new people, they were tied to a mortgage and strapped with weekend maintenance that drained their energy and wallets.

Then came Tiny Homes! Suddenly, instead of spending your lives' savings to keep up with the Jones's living in a 3,000-square foot home, you could be trendy living in a 200-square foot Tiny Home. No more worries about a tight job market or being laid off by a downsizing corporation, Tiny Homeowners can simply roll their homes to a neighboring town with better career prospects and greater opportunities. There are such beauty and ease in Tiny Home living, with no more money lost in selling and buying homes or worry about packing—just move. Viola! You've got your life back; you're in control and loving every minute of it.

Life Doesn't Have to be so Difficult

Isn't it strange how we've learned to complicate our lives so much? In the stone age, we were hunters and gathers to survive. Although we have evolved, just how far have we come? We still hunt, but the hunt is for a simpler life, and we're eager to rid ourselves of all the useless trinkets and gadgets we have gathered along the way to clutter our lives and compromise our freedom. If you often feel nostalgic and long to jump off the merry-go-round some call success, welcome to what could be your new life in a Tiny Home.

Deciding to change your lifestyle doesn't have to be that difficult. If you're entertaining the idea of a Tiny Home, you owe it to yourself to do a little homework, and you've come to the right place to start. Once you begin reading about what it takes to build and maintain a Tiny Home and you talk to those who have already made the jump, you have more clarity on what it entails. Don't be fooled, Tiny Home living is not for everybody, but it could be for you. You won't know if you don't investigate the possibilities.

To be fair, there are some challenges to the process, so going into it with your eyes wide open is the best. It's only difficult to make the decision to live in a Tiny Home when you have failed to prepare or when you haven't looked at all the potential barriers, so let's identify some of those, shall we?

Examining the Downside to Tiny Homes

Let's face it, no matter how adventurous you might feel, it's a scary thing to make such a radical change. The best way to deal with fear is to face it head on and make an informed, healthy decision rather than one that is generated by fear.

The Fear of Change

Most people have become very attached to their material things, and the thought of losing those things can be quite frightening. Another fear can be just the loss of space. Tiny Homes are—well—tiny. Everything must have its place and be put back there if you are to have room to move around comfortably in the Tiny Home. People who are claustrophobic will most likely not be joining the Tiny Homes movement. Still, others fear their bigger size might prevent them from maneuvering within the limited space of a Tiny Home; however, today's space-saving furnishings have taken that into allowance, and we'll be discussing that more in another chapter. You'll know soon enough whether your fears are warranted or you can put them to rest once you investigate a bit further what it's like to live tiny.

There might also be some fear as to what your family and friends might have to say should you decide to be a Tiny homeowner. In the long run, Tiny Home living is a choice you should only make after carefully researching all the pros and cons. Then, make the decision that's right for you, no matter what others say. After all, your lifestyle should be your choice and reflect your desires and priorities, so let anybody stand in your way if you discover that owning a Tiny Home is perfect for the next chapter of your life.

Finding a Place to Put Your Tiny Home

It might sound simple enough, but finding land or a place to put your Tiny Home can be your greatest challenge in owning one. If you decide to buy land and live in a Tiny Home until your property is paid for, that's one thing. On the other hand, if you want an entirely debt-free lifestyle, then you're going to need a place to park the thing. If you want to be closer to the city, then you'll have to find a small piece of land that won't break the bank and yet be zoned to allow a Tiny Home. Or, you might have a friend with property who's willing to allow you to occupy a small piece for a token amount of money each month.

If your plan is to live out in the sticks, you'll need to know ahead of time so that you can design your Tiny Home to be self-sustainable. Properties or raw land that is farther out most likely won't have power or water, so you'll need to design some eco-friendly features in your home that will allow you to function. Since Tiny Homes don't have much of a footprint, the only concern might be to make sure you have some vegetation covering for privacy, perhaps solar power and a small generator is good for your power supply.

Parking outside the city limits won't ensure you settlers' rights. If your plan is to travel lightly and quietly, living covertly in the woods, then you'll need nature to provide a refuge for your Tiny Home until you're ready to move to the next location. The best plan is to make sure your Tiny Home sits on land and that you comply with the law.

Is Your Tiny Home an Investment or a Depreciating Liability?

For most lending institutions, Tiny Homes are considered a personal property that depreciates. If you need to get a loan on your Tiny Home, you'll most likely be asked for a substantial amount down, and be prepared that many lenders will just refuse your request for a loan altogether. That's the reason why many owners save for years to pay cash or why they build their Tiny Home over the course of a year or more, paying as they go.

If you have excellent credit, you might want to put your home on several credit cards, and then pay them down in the following years. Of course, the interest will be more, but look at what you'll save by not have a conventional mortgage. If you currently own a large home outright or have a good deal of equity in your home, then it's possible for you to sell your home or take out an equity loan and pay cash for your Tiny Home.

Whatever your decision, there's attraction to Tiny Home living that cannot be denied. It's created a shift in many people's paradigms of what they previously considered to be living the "good life." If your curiosity has got the best of you, then keep reading. It might just be that there is a Tiny Home for you in your future.

Chapter 3: The Eco-Friendly Benefits

Tiny Homes might be small, but their advantages are enormous! For many people, living in a Tiny Home means financial well-being; for others, it means they have the freedom to be mobile and live where they want when they want. Then, there are those people whose concerns are for the planet as much as for their wallet. You don't need to be a '70s hippie or a tree-hugger to understand that people are consuming far more of the earth's resources than can be replaced. When we see clear evidence of global warming, the erosion of our ozone, and the sad extinction of our wildlife, it's no wonder those concerned about the planet are turning to Tiny Homes. It's quite eye opening how much each Tiny Home saves and protects our earth.

If you're entertaining the wisdom of investing in a Tiny Home, maybe the following facts will help you hurdle some of your obstacles and give it a try. Not only do Tiny Homes tear down personal living costs, but they also significantly reduce the impact that construction waste, lumber squandering, and the over-the-top emission of CO_2 into our atmosphere. Let's break this down a bit further, shall we?

Tiny Homes Minimize Construction Waste

Approximately 40% of our planet's solid waste, in one way or another, is generated by construction. It's jaw-dropping how much of a difference in waste occurs when building a Tiny Home of about 200–300 square feet to that of a regular home of around 2,600 square feet. Between framing, tiling, sheathing, roofing, siding, and concrete, a close approximation of waste for a Tiny Home is 400 pounds, while you can expect to haul about 5,000 USD of waste from a regular-sized home. Even Tiny Home Builders who aren't being particularly conscious of using reclaimed materials experience these differences first-hand. The Tiny Home dweller can provide evidence showing just a simple build has a big difference due to home size alone.

Timber Usage Minimized in a Tiny Home

In the United States, almost three-quarters of the entire consumption of timber each year is from the private housing industry. While it's admirable to recycle paper products, it can't begin to make the dent in timber usage that building a Tiny Home can. It takes more than 90% more wood to build a 2,600-square foot home than it does to build a 200-square foot Tiny Home. Using less timber means less power to cut, age, split, finish, store, and haul. What could be hauled in a few hours to build a Tiny Home might take repeated trips over several days to drag on the building site of a regular-sized home. Therefore, building Tiny Homes also saves on diesel gas as well as fossil fuel.

Comparing the Emissions of CO2

The release of CO2 into the earth's atmosphere has played havoc with our global climate, and it is considered the most active participants in the creation of global warming. Although some politicians would like to pretend that global warming doesn't exist, science paints an entirely different picture of its effects. Global warming has caused our ice caps to recede and our seas to rise. Our wildlife habitats have been devastated by global warming, causing over a million-different species to become extinct and bringing others to the brink of extinction.

Almost 18% of the earth's greenhouse gasses are emitted from the private housing industry at an astronomical rate. A 3,000-square foot house will emit 28,000 pounds of CO2 per year into the earth's atmosphere, as opposed to only 2,000 pounds of CO2 per year from a Tiny Home. While being elegantly small, Tiny Homes are incredibly efficient, using only 914 kWh of electricity per year compared to 12,773 kWh per year in a regular-sized build. It doesn't take rocket science to figure out that the savings in electricity, heating, and cooling of your Tiny Home is going to be positively reflected in your monthly finances as well.

Eco-Friendly Devices and Practices

There are things Tiny Home dwellers regularly do that allows them to be totally "off the grid" and live in harmony with their environment. Most of the time, these aren't extraordinary measures taken by Tiny Homeowners, but rather, it is the norm for them. We have listed some of these eco-friendly devices and practices so that you can get an idea of the Tiny Home lifestyle.

Composting Toilet

A compost toilet is a waterless system that uses an aerobic process to decompose human excrement. The best composting toilets divert the urine from the solids and then use a fan run by a generator to dry the solid waste further. If the bathroom works well and the device is proper, there will be no odor, and the waste can be used to fertilize a garden or plants. Depending on how many people are living in your Tiny Home, the toilet will need to be emptied and cleaned out about every 3 to 4 weeks.

Although composting toilets will save you about $50 a month on your water bill if you are hooked up to city services, the initial cost of a compost toilet can be much more expensive. While the expense of a flushing toilet is a price of $100 to

$200, a composting toilet will cost about $1,500 to $4,000. This device is not done to save the Tiny Home dweller money, but to allow them to be self-sustainable and not depend on public services.

Before you decide on a composting toilet, if you are living in the city, be sure to check with city codes—some prohibit their use within the city limits. If a composting toilet is your choice, you can also dilute the urine and turn it into the gray water for use in the garden. Dried solid waste can be utilized for that purpose as well.

Solar and Wind Power

Using the earth as a resource to power your Tiny Home is commonly achieved, but don't think it's going to cost you next to nothing. It's initially much more expensive to construct your Tiny Home using eco-friendly devices, but there's a beauty in doing so. You can live in the middle of nowhere, entirely independent of any outside services and their costs. Throughout the years, these eco-friendly devices will pay for themselves, and allow you the freedom that few have; however, if you are working on a limited budget, it might take a while to purchase and implement these systems.

Solar cells and the wind can totally power a Tiny Home. You'll first need to decide the size of your Tiny Home and how many people will be living in it. Then, you'll need to determine what will be run from your Tiny Home. For instance, will your stove be gas or electric? How much water will you need to heat in an average day? Will the area where you'll be living provide sufficient sun rays and wind? If not, how big a generator will you need? There are lots of questions to be answered, and the answers vary on your private use of the Tiny Home.

You might need a solar calculator to determine the number of solar panels needed to provide power. Once you have calculated the number of solar cells, then decide whether you can install them on the roof of your home or you'll need some free-standing panels. Wherever you place your solar panels, be sure to keep them out of the way of trees or shrubs that might block the sun or damage them. Depending on your needs, wind power can be accomplished by installing a rooftop wind turbine.

The following is a creative design that shows built-in solar cells that coat the rooftop and a wind turbine attached to the capsule. Although this is an ultra-modern design currently being used more for research and commercial office space in remote areas, it just might be the wave of the future for Tiny Home dwellers.

Gray Water and Rain Water Harvesting System

Most areas are not going to have enough rainfall to provide all the water you'll need each month, but a substantial amount can be harvested before having to tap into your backup supply. If your Tiny Home is going to be stationary, then you might want to consider a sizeable cistern to store rainwater. The average water needs are as follows.

Drinking Water Per Person   1 Gallon

Toilet (if flushable)   2 Gallons Per Flush

Shower   2 Gallons Per Minute

Of course, this does not include the water needed for cooking or washing your hands, dishes, and clothing. If we assume the average conservative adult will use 15 gallons of water a day, that would require approximately four inches of rainfall a month. Naturally, the water needs will increase for each additional person living in the Tiny Home. In most locations, rain doesn't fall each day or month equally, so it is necessary to have a storage device. One such device is a rain pillow.

This one is large and can be stored outside, if weather permits, but you can also get them in all sizes to conveniently fit beneath a bed or under a cabinet as well. Since they are inflatable, they are easy to empty and store when you are on the move.

Propane Power

Propane tanks are easy to install in a Tiny Home. One of the things to be aware of is that warm-climate propane is different than the cold-climate one. The butane levels are higher in cold-climates. It's a good practice to always use the propane in the area to which you purchased it. If not, trade in your tanks and buy new when you relocate. The propane is usually attached outside on the trailer or the side of a stationary Tiny Home.

Propane will supply power to things like a gas stove and electricity, should your solar and wind power not be adequate, to heat your water. It can also run your air conditioning and heating as well.

Building Green

During the building process, you'll want to make use of all the repurposed and reclaimed supplies possible. For insulation, wood construction, and storage space within your Tiny Home, using reclaimed and repurposed materials will help you do your part to protect the planet. Because your needs will be smaller in size, much of your building supplies can be obtained from other larger-sized building sites. Visit your local builder and ask if you can salvage scrap from their builds. Most will be happy to help and appreciate the time and money saved to haul their wasted building products to a construction dump. (BUT DO NOT STEAL MATERIALS)

These are just a few of the items to consider if your desire is to live off the grid or to go green as much as possible. Although it's much easier to install these products during your build, if a limited budget holds you back, you can always do a little at a time. Every little bit counts in resources consumed and money saved.

Chapter 4: Smart Storage

When people are deciding whether to live tiny, one of the biggest issues is whether they'll be able to live with less stuff. We are all incredible accumulators of stuff. We have too much stuff to wear, watch, maintain, and pay for in our lives. Some people judge their worth by their stuff; they compare their stuff with other people's stuff to see who has the best stuff. Others brag about their stuff by placing invisible pricing stickers on their cars (a brand/badge) saying how they believe their stuff is better than your stuff.

No doubt, there isn't one of us who couldn't do without about 70% of our stuff. If that's the case, most of us would be okay living in a Tiny Home. The problem then becomes what stuff to get rid of in the process. Along with doing away with all the stuff we don't use, we can also be better organizers of the limited space offered in a Tiny Home. To maximize every nook and cranny, let's discuss smart ways to use space for both living and storage in a Tiny Home.

Smart Storage Ideas

Smart storage can be built right into the design of your Tiny Home, or you can choose to keep several storage containers mobile, so they double as seats, tables, beds, and desks. Most Tiny Homes have breakfast tables that double as office desks and benches that have storage beneath them as well. Below are a few ideas that people have used to open their space when they are not eating or sleeping. They are little pods—when pushed together, they create a spacious and comfortable sectional for you and company. Or, when separated, they act as dining chairs, support for a table or bed.

The more moveable the furnishings, the more flexible the space. The same room can be your living room, dining room, and entertainment area. You might need to get used to keeping your linens in a room other than the bathroom, and your clothing somewhere besides your bedroom. You just find a suitable spot to store whatever fits where.

Above are some ways builders have used the space below and within the stairs of a Tiny Home. Using each stair as storage for clothing and linens is a wonderful way to maximize that space. On the photo to the right, you'll notice that the builder has also used the space below the stairs to place a stackable washer and dryer. When using stairs as storage, be careful not to design and build them too steep for easy climbing and too high for easy access. Always follow the building code of stairs when building, so get a stair maker to measure up or follow these rules if you think you are capable of building them yourself. But remember if you are to sell this home and you have built the stairs yourself you are liable for up to 7 years for them as you did the renovation as an <u>Owner builder</u>.

The staircase should comply with these rules:

- The top of the handrail must be located between 34 and 38-inches (860 and 970-mm) above the pitch line.
- Along any open side of a stairway, the balusters must be located such that a 4-3/8-inch (110 mm) sphere cannot pass through.
- The riser height is limited to 7-3/4 inches (200 mm).
- A minimum tread depth of 10 inches (250 mm) is required, measured horizontally between the nosings of adjacent treads.
- The headroom clearance along any point of the must be at least 80-inches (2 meters).

Walls in a Tiny Home are not just for beautiful pictures and interesting ornaments; they're for storage. Although some builders have such creative ideas that they've combined the two—design with room to create a beautiful space with color, style, and functionality.

You'll notice the containers for food storage as well as the alcoves on the far wall that can be used for books, vases, dishes, or various other needs. Not only are the containers useful for storing food, but the top doubles as a shelf for dishes.

In the images below you see how talented builders have utilized that awkward space that's always left between the refrigerator and wall. Instead of using it as an empty dust collector, they've designed a pullout shelf to hold small things like spices. In the picture to the right, you can see how one Tiny Home dweller turns a beautiful desk into a table with two benches. You might also notice how much of the furniture in a Tiny Home is light and airy to prevent that closed-in feeling of the darker woods and heavier furniture. For example, the two benches for the dining table are conveniently stored beneath the desk when they are not in use.

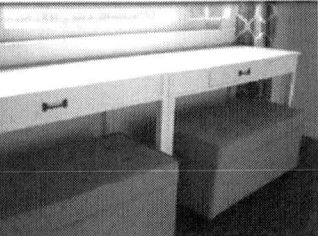

Depending upon the placement of the kitchen to the stairs, some have used the sides of the stairs for storage rather than the front. The longer shelves are convenient for storing dishes or pots and pans and can be covered or closed by using doors. The wider door that includes the two more extended shelves could be hinged and folded out to use as a table top. The only thing that limits the number of storage areas a Tiny House contains is one's imagination.

This wide-open sectional room offers the homeowner a lot of room to stretch out or lounge, but it can also function as a dining or game table by rearranging the squares.

In the picture above, you can see how the table or desk has been folded up to the wall to allow for additional walking space (instead of paining it the same color as the wall you could potentially get it painted as a nice painting). There are also nooks at the end of the kitchen counter to hold a coffee pot and dishes. The important thing to remember is that in a Tiny Home, everything has its place. If you don't use the storage you have, Tiny Homes can look cluttered and become uncomfortably tight.

Most Tiny Houses have smart storage using a lot of vertical wall space, as shown below. If necessary, you can hide a small stool to be used to reach the higher drawers and shelves. You'll also notice on the photo below how there is a drop shelf on the ceiling to store lighter objects and further utilize the vertical space.

The sleeping loft has been placed over the sofa, maximizing living space on both the bottom floor and the loft. But if you are to store clothing or shoes in shelved areas I strongly suggest installing doors or draws as it makes the room look neater and less cluttered.

Under the Floor and Between the Studs Space

Most builders don't recommend putting storage areas under the floor or between the studs in the walls because of moisture problems and difficulties in accessing the items. However, there are still a lot of people who choose to use these areas. If you decide to include some in your Tiny Home, remember to insulate the containers well and only store things in these areas that would not be damaged by a little additional moisture.

Use your vertical space well, keeping shelves and drawers narrow to ensure they dont protrude out too far into your living space. If you make some of your storage moveable as shown in some of the pictures, you should have plenty of room to store all the things you'll need in your Tiny Home.

When Things Get Too Crowded

Living in a larger home gives you the luxury of keeping unnecessary items for years without bothering to do spring cleaning. In fact, many people have boxes in their garage or shed that they couldn't remember the contents of to save their lives. If they were given $1000 to name what was inside the box, they'd be hard put even to name the general items it contains.

In a Tiny Home, you don't have that luxury. There are no forgotten boxes stored in the garage because you don't have a garage. Most people living in a Tiny Home use every item in their home on a regular basis. They cannot afford to abide by the 3-year rule: you know, if you haven't used an item in 3 years, get rid of it. Their rule is more like a 3-month rule.

You have a few more options when you plan on being stationary in your Tiny Home. For example, you could store extra things in a used shipping container right next to your

Tiny Home. They are water tight and sturdily built, and they could hold things that are infrequently used, such as sporting equipment and camping gear.

If you fear feelings of claustrophobia, you can always build in a few more windows. Just remember, the more windows you have, the less vertical space you'll have to use for storage. Windows make a Tiny House open and bring the outside in, but we'll talk about that in the next chapter.

The Bathroom Storage Challenge in Tiny Homes

Bathrooms are one of the most challenging spaces in a Tiny Home, especially if two or more people need to share the space. There needs to be room for cosmetics, blow dryer, hair care products, shaving things, and medicine. All these requirements and still creating room for a mirror, tub, shower, and toilet can be this side of impossible if you aren't a spatial guru. If you plan before the build and you're creative, you can achieve success.

For instance, some have built tubs with removable panels and storage beneath. These areas can be great useful spaces if your items are plastic and not susceptible to damage from moisture. You can store bottles of shampoo, conditioner, soap, cleaning products, cotton swabs, a safety kit, and various other items. It's also common to see bathroom doors that are a little thicker and have open shelving on one side for toiletry items.

If you have a counter next to your bathroom sink, don't waste the space beneath it. Close it in and create storage for cosmetics, blow dryers, and shaving supplies. You might want to hang your wet towels outside to dry instead of taking up room in the bathroom for towel racks. If you live in the woods, you could decide to have an outdoor shower attached to your Tiny Home and reserve the bathroom space for beautifying yourself.

A Changed Perspective in Tiny Living

If you want to have plenty of storage, it begins before you even build your Tiny Home. It starts with changing your way of thinking before changing your lifestyle. Don't try to move all the things from a large home into a Tiny Home. Sort through everything several times before paring down your items. It's best to divide those things into four categories.

1. Things you don't need and can give away.

2. Things you would like but could do without if necessary.

3. Things you need to have in your Tiny Home.

4. And things that can be kept in a separate storage area outside.

Your first few sort throughs should be to get rid of the things that you haven't used for years and had forgotten you owned. If you're a clutter bug, these first few cleanouts will get rid of at least 60% of the things you don't need.

Next, there will be the things you would like to take with you but that you could live without if space were a prohibiting factor. Much of these things might be sentimental, so maybe you could ask a relative to store them for you. Try to avoid getting a storage unit and using it to just switch all the unnecessary things from your large home to a storage locker. If this is your plan, you might as well continue to pay a mortgage. Instead, be honest with yourself and ask yourself the following five questions.

1. Why do I need this item?

2. Does someone need it or would they appreciate it more than me?

3. How would I feel if I didn't have this item any longer?

4. What would I need to leave behind if I took this with me? Is it worth it?

5. How do I plan on using it in my Tiny House?

There are some items you have emotional feelings for, but you might find that there is no use or need for them with your changed lifestyle. You could sell them and use the money to purchase something that would make your life more enjoyable in your Tiny home, like a hammock, outdoor furniture, or bicycles. Tiny living gives you a lot more time for pleasure and enjoyment, and most Tiny Home dwellers find themselves spending that time on outdoor adventures.

You just need to change your thinking before changing your lifestyle and your home. You can do with a lot less or perhaps different things that will bring you more contentment in your Tiny Home. Not to worry—you'll find the perfect place to store those things you are most passionate about, and that bring you

Chapter 5: How To Build a Tiny House Following The Building Stages

There are many ideas and styles of building a tiny home. But if you are wanting to do as much of this as you can in your spare time, then we will work through this together to help you get an idea of what it is exactly that you need to be doing.

Planning stage:

First of all, we need to think about what style of Tiny House you are after... Do you want a self-sufficient Tiny home that you can tow around or do you want to build a self-sufficient tiny home that's going to be non-movable?

When purchasing your land or trailer, for this stage you need to look into what area you want to be living in and how big you want your home to be. You may be thinking 'well I want a tiny home that is movable but I have no idea how big I actually want it'?

The best way to decide this is to go into a trailer company's yard and have a look at the different sizes they have. This will allow you to get an idea of what size you are after. Remember to keep in mind the car you drive and don't get a trailer that your vehicle cannot tow.

But if you're building a non-moveable home then size isn't that much of an issue, as you are building it on land. But it is still important to sit down and think about what items you actually need and how small you can build your home to make it livable, because here we are not building a normal sized home, we are building a tiny home to reduce all costs of living.

Once you have purchased your land through a real estate agency or a trailer through a trusted trailer company then we are ready for the next stage.

Design stage:

Now that we have land or a trailer we need to focus on the design. Designing a new home is always exciting, but we need to gather information and picture designs of different homes to give us a true idea of what we want. The best way to do this is to browse on the internet by typing in "Tiny Houses" or finding magazines within your local news agency or book store.

Once you have filled a book or folder with different images and designs that you would like your tiny home to look like, you are ready to take it to a draftsman or an architect. Most people generally don't know a draftsman or architect, but don't worry, just talk to your builder friends or look online for a trusted professional.

Now that you have had your dream Tiny House designed you are ready to get the necessary permits if you are going to build your home on a block of land.

For this, you will need to contact your local council and find out all of the appropriate permits you are required to have or contact a builder in your local area. Because if you do not get the correct permits and you just build a home where you want you may be looking at large fines or your home removed (if caught).

Foundation stage:
Once you have your plans and permits in place for your home, you can start with the foundations of your home. For this it once again depends on what type of home your building; non-movable or movable.

If you are building your home on a trailer you want to build a sub floor on top of the trailer so you are able to crane your home off of the trailer if needed. This will be your foundations, and you want your sub floor to be built in a way that you are able to have it lifted. For this I suggest adding in extra bearers to allow for the movement of the home.

Alternatively, for your non-movable you need to have your foundations designed for the specific soil or ground that you are going to put your house on.

The footings or slab are the foundations of what your home will be sitting on, hence you need to ensure that it is 100% stable. To do so you must have the plans in hand that have been written by an engineer, because they consider the soils grade and what type of foundation is required for your block of land where you are building the home. Sometimes the engineer will allow two types of foundations depending of your grade of soil and how much weight your home will bear, (if it's a 3-story tiny home you will need bigger and stronger footings).

A major risk involved with this is that you don't listen to the engineer and you get the cheapest option of foundation, you may find that your tiny home is now on a drastic lean and you have to get all the water, electrical and layers of your home disassembled and re-assembled years down the track.

Wall Frame stage:

At frame stage, you need to follow all specifications that your designer has created when it is regarding anything structural and load bearing. But if you decide to change the size of an internal wall later, that is ok as long as it doesn't carry any load from the side walls. When doing the frame, you will need to hire a carpenter unless you are in fact a carpenter because the frame is a critical part of your house. If you think you can do it and you do it incorrectly it can cause a lot of injury to you or a loved one. It is more important with the movable home because it is constantly moving which can cause weaknesses in the structure.

One tip to framing though is to ensure you always have a minimum of two people doing it because you will always need someone to give you materials while you are on a ladder. The trick to carpentry is to always be productively moving, if you are on your own you will take 3 times as long compared to if you have a second person. This is due to unnecessary movements getting up and down ladders or thinking of different ways to lift heavy materials alone. As opposed to having a second person lift with you and save a lot of time.

Roof stage:

Once the wall frame is built, we need to build the roof. This will allow us to then work on the external cladding of the frame without water damaging the materials. For the roof of a portable house you will normally require it to be tin because it is light weight and we need to restrict the amount of weight we load on our trailer.

The easiest way to have a roof built is to order roof trusses from a 'roof truss company' and then have carpenters build the roof according to the plan. You can purchase and order this yourself if you want to save money on material costs. Just give the house plans to the truss company and they will come onsite and measure up to ensure that everything will work.

Then from there you just need to have the carpenters put the roof battens on, for the roof plumbers to screw the tin roof down, and install the guttering.

Now here comes the eco-friendly part of your home, after the roof is complete we can buy and install the solar panels to allow for solar panel lighting/heating and cooling. Ensure that your electricians have already accounted for this before they start the 'rough in' because we want our main energy supply to run off of our solar panels. This is an expensive purchase to begin with but we will make all of that money back after the first 3 years of owning the home.

External cladding stage:

You will be organizing/building the outside walls of your home now. Most tiny homes are made from timber cladding (timber weather boards) because they are cheaper and look more effective on a small home. Once again for this process you will need a carpenter or if you think you can do it yourself go ahead, but make sure that you don't waste more time and money than what you would be earning with your current job.

Also, another extremely beneficial product to add onto your tiny home is a tank water service that captures all of the rain water off of your roof, so you can add that onto the side of your home here in this stage after the external cladding is done and your home is completely weather proof.

Lock up stage:

Lock up stage is a mixture of jobs to get the frame ready for plaster.

This will include:

- Getting an electrician in to do the start of the wiring, commonly known as a 'rough in' this is where they cut holes in your frame and run all of the wires ready to be fitted off later in the build. I recommend getting an electrician.
- Getting a plumber in to do the start of the plumbing, also commonly known as a 'rough in' this is where they cut holes in your frame and run all of the pipes ready to be fitted off later in the build. I recommend getting a plumber.

- Straightening walls using a straight edge, timber packers and a planer to get rid of all bumps in the timber walls. To allow plaster to go on the walls without bumps.
- Installing the insulation within the walls and ceiling to reduce heat loss and help withhold the cool or hot air in your home.
- Installing stairs, if you have them and it is a double or triple story home

Plastering stage:

Now that everything is ready for plaster we can order and hang the plaster. This is an easy job that we can all do ourselves. You'll just need a strong friend or two and a screw gun that plasterers use.

For plastering you just need to watch a few videos on YouTube to gain the knowledge of what to do. You should be able to hang the plaster sheets on the walls and roof yourself if you're a physically capable person. But then to get a professional finish I suggest getting a plasterer in to do the 'stopping up' (getting rid of the joins in the plaster).

Fit off / more lockup and fix Stage:

The fit off stage is described simply as just connecting all of the electrical and plumbing services, then completing the final stages of the carpentry. For this process you will be just finishing all of the above and your carpenter will install any doors, architraves, skirtings, cupboards or cabinets.

Painting:

Now we get to do the fun part of painting. Painting is a matter of getting the colors you like, then making sure you roll/ brush everything evenly. Painting is not that hard, it's quite relaxing but it is definitely a skill to get everything neat and perfect when it comes down to the fine line. You need to focus on making sure everything is neat when you do it and use long smooth brush strokes all going in one direction. The best way to paint is up and down the walls and not left and right horizontally because the paint may want to drip downwards. Also make sure to use painters masking tape on the windows and doors where you do not want to paint.

Flooring:

Now that all of the messy jobs are done we just need to install the type of flooring coverings that we want. Depending on if you want tiles, carpet or floor boards I suggest you get the appropriate tradesman in to do those tasks unless you have the knowledge and capabilities to do so yourself.

Finishing:

Now we do all of the finishing steps to the build. Now we install all of the door handles door stops, appliances, kitchen stove top, foldable beds and draws that will be hidden under stair cases (anything that is a finishing touch). Normally the staining of floor boards and laying carpet are the last two big steps.

Now you will have a completed tiny house built to your exact style that is ecofriendly and self-sufficient.

Carpentry and Building advice:

Remember throughout a whole build if you can purchase the materials and have them delivered to site you will save at least 15% on you're build. This is due to the fact that most builders always add 10-15% mark up on materials. Then if you are extremely switched on, you will also be going to builder's auctions in order to get cheap materials that were spares from other people's jobs or miss ordered. If you're interested in the idea of saving money then this would be well worth your time, to look up online where the nearest builder's auctions are and go bid on different materials that you will need for your job. You have the potential of saving up to another 15%!!!

Chapter 6: Design Dynamics and Building Plans

There are many ideas and styles, but the best thing to design for yourself in a Tiny Home is a new lifestyle. As you make this incredible change to reside in a Tiny Home, you need to make it a point to change your lifestyle as well. Get outdoors more, and give yourself time to enjoy life. We spend a lifetime being two-minded—worried about our home life when we're at work and worried about work when we're supposed to be giving our families our undivided attention. For some reason, living in a Tiny Home makes you more relaxed and focused on the good things in life. Maybe it's because you don't have as many other distractions like bills, debt, and all that work to maintain a larger home. Or maybe it is that in the tiny home you have less commercial items that make you think it's more about what you have not who you have.

Okay, so you've decided to design a better life for yourself. One of the first things that should concern you while building your Tiny Home is safety. Tiny Homes fall in that category. Even though they can be on wheels and resemble an RV type vehicle, they are not required to meet any RV safety standards. Those that are married to the land, or stationary, are rarely regulated by any city or building codes or inspections. While this sounds great to free-spirited Tiny Home dwellers, it could mean serious injury or even death should they fail to take the proper precautions when designing their Tiny Homes.

Building Lofts and Stairs

Predominately everybody's concern about the loft and the stairs is that they take the most space in a Tiny Home. Of course, you want to give yourself as much space to roam as possible, but you won't be going anywhere if you're flat on your back with an injury. So, here are a few things to keep in mind when building a loft and stairs. Take a look at the interior photo of the Tiny Home below, and let's see if they followed some basic safety standards.

Looking at the loft, they have taken the proper precautions about making sure there are sturdy railings to protect sleepers in the loft from rolling off and onto the floor in their sleep. Children are especially prone to this, which would be quite a drop for them. Many lofts have no rails at all, and you'll often see people sitting up in the loft with their feet dangling over the edge. If they should try to prop themselves up and slip, they could go tumbling to the floor—head first.

What else about the loft do you see that has been done well? The ceilings have adequate space to sit upright without bumping one's head. Some have a clearance of less than 2 feet, which could create an issue if you needed to vacate the loft in a hurry or even just sit up too fast. Although it will cost more money, having higher clearance in your loft will be worth it in the long run. You'll be more comfortable and much safer.

Another issue that many have when they build lofts is the window size. You'll notice that there are a couple of windows in this loft, and they are all large enough for one to exit them should there be a fire that prevented them from going down the stairs. Although those little round porthole windows are stylish from a designer's point of view, they're a death trap if there were to be a fire. So, make sure you have at least one window in your loft that is large enough for everybody who will be sleeping there to get through in case of fire. Two large windows in the loft would be ideal if we want to go overboard on the safety.

As we come down the stairs now, do they look safe? They are not so steep that one would have trouble climbing them safely, and they have guard rails for protection against an accidental slip. The stairs also look broad enough to fit your entire foot on as you climb, which offers greater support and a much more secure climb.

As we move down the stairs, there is something that should catch your eye. It's the heater placed directly across from the gas stove. Whenever possible, try to keep your propane items away from fire elements and protected from extreme temperatures.

One more thing—can you guess? The interior consists of knotty pine, which can act like kindling in a fire. Knotty pine would not be an approved material for an RV, but Tiny Homes are not held to the same standards. Just be sure if you choose to build with highly combustible wood throughout your Tiny Home, you should have plenty of ventilation and smoke alarms. When you purchase appliances that use gas or are wood-burning fixtures, make sure they are RV approved for safety purposes.

Now that we've protected you, what about protecting your Tiny Home? Make sure you have insurance on your Tiny Home. You wouldn't drive a car without insurance, and you shouldn't live in a Tiny Home without being covered. It's just too much money to invest without the reassurance that you'd be able to rebuild and replace items in case of an accident or damage. You should be especially concerned if you're mobile. You don't want to be driving your house through the major cities and taking the chance that some lunatic driver is going to run into your home, right?

Creative Designs

Green Builder Media, Shelter Dynamics, Kitcheneering, and Align3D developed the Tiny Home you see next. They named it "The Arches House," and it's easy to understand why. These designer/builders soon recognized that Tiny Homes built with arches give the illusion of a lot more space. If nothing else, they are much more interesting and creative. The curving arches were carried from the exterior through to the interior design as well, giving the home continuity and harmony.

From ceiling to hallway beams, the interior supports the entire theme of the Tiny Home, enabling it to blend beautifully with its surroundings.

Another example of how incredible the curve looks is the Tiny Home below. The curve was an easy one to achieve in this Tiny Home because it is a remodel of an old warehouse building. They supported it with curved beams and even curved the stairs, but we would have liked to see them finish the stairs with a handrail. The loft looks dark, so we weren't sure if there were windows up there. Again, you should be noticing features like these for safety and aesthetics.

Both homes have made good use of the sun's rays by designing their Tiny Homes with a myriad of windows. Windows keep Tiny Home dwellers from feeling cooped up, but safety is an issue to be concerned about here as well. If you are living in an extreme climate with lots of rain and heavy winds, make sure you have used double-paned windows that are properly fit to resist moisture. If you have a tendency to place your Tiny Home near tall trees, you'll want to be sure they are not a hazard in high winds.

These photos are meant to get your creative juices flowing and open your mind to all the possibilities in a Tiny Home. However, it's clear that many of these features will be costly. If you've decided on a Tiny Home for financial freedom, you'll want to continue to keep your budget in the forefront as you plan your design. But in saying that you are reducing your homes size dramatically so don't be too stingy on the cost or you will end up with a very simplistic home that doesn't look aesthetically pleasing inside and out. Which then has the cause of effect of discomfort and dissatisfaction of your own home.

The interior shot below displays a design with very high ceilings, which makes the home look and feel that much larger. The kitchen area was located beneath the loft for maximum space in the living area. There are also lots of large windows in this Tiny Home, giving it the appearance of being open and spacious. Making use of all the natural light will also cut down on the homeowner's unnecessary use of lights.

Tiny Home Floorplans

To provide some ideas on space and room placement, we've included the following floorplans.

This is an impressive floorplan showing a rare two-bedroom Tiny Home. This home has a double loft, with one bedroom over the kitchen and the other over the living room.

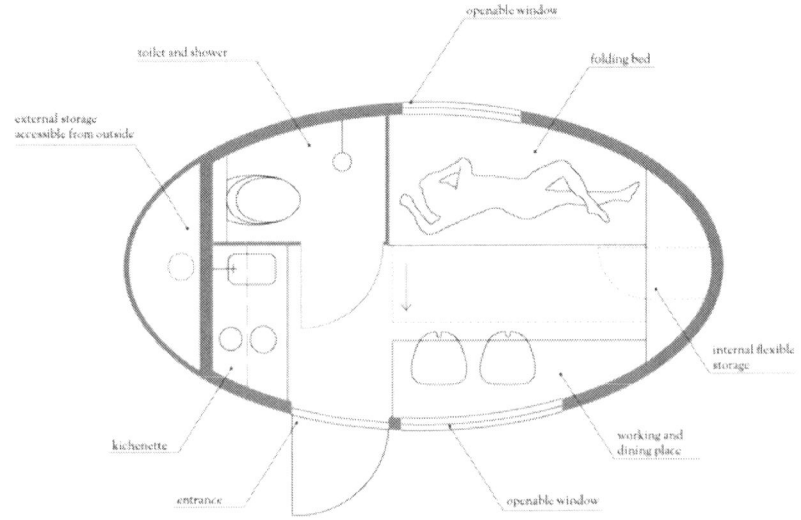

Again, you will see the interesting use of curves in this capsule Tiny Home. It has a clean, minimalist design and has used white walls, furnishings, and light wood cabinets and fixtures to keep the capsule house looking open and welcoming.

Not only did the following Tiny Home use curves for design appeal, but it also used color and local materials to keep the home in harmony with its surroundings. Whenever you can use local building materials or reclaimed materials from the area, it will help to make your Tiny Home seem as though it was built with that area in mind. Notice the thatched room and the stone walkway, all local and natural materials that blend nicely with the location of the Tiny Home.

Colors, shapes, and textures all add to your design and give it your individual signature. Since Tiny Homes are expected to look unique and just a bit quirky, it's perfectly okay to let your imagination run wild. Who knows, your Tiny Home might be featured on television or in a magazine touting wonderfully designed homes.

To create your space and unique features, you can also take a look at several free software programs you can download and use to get a rough sketch of your Tiny Home. Some are quite sophisticated, with 3D planning tools and easy to use full imaging, that can create an accurate picture of how your Tiny Home will look.

The best thing about designing your Tiny Home is exploring and experimenting with space and features. As well as making it safe, functional, and beautiful—there's one more thing. Have a great time when designing your Tiny Home! Because you are now becoming a designer for the time being and you want a home to be proud of still.

Chapter 7: Quotes for a New Home Build

The range of prices for which you can build a Tiny Home is as varied as the homes themselves. It all depends on what you are looking for in your Tiny Home. If you're working on a limited budget, then it is possible to build a Tiny Home for less than $10,000. If you are looking for a cheap and trendy style with everything new, then building your Tiny Home could run you $35,000 plus. The first thing to do is to decide on your budget because that will determine what your Tiny Home will cost and what materials you will look to use. We'll give you examples of both so you can see the difference.

A Tiny Home Built for Less than $10,000

The average cost to build a Tiny Home is $25,000, so you know it took some work and time to make this one for under $10,000. This Tiny Home is 24 feet long, 8 feet wide, and 13 feet tall. The following are some of its features.

- Composting toilet, tub and shower together, and bathroom sink
- Refrigerator—not full size
- Double sinks in kitchen
- Dishwasher
- Gas range—full size
- Pantry—large
- Two lofts—one fits a king-size bed and the other a twin size bed
- Solid stairs—no ladder
- Living area with 7-foot sofa
- Lots of windows and storage
- Vinyl siding on exterior
- Tongue and groove hardwood flooring

To build on the cheap without it looking like you did, plan on spending more time to look for bargains and then a place to store the things you find. When you find a deal, you need to purchase and pick it up right then. Waiting only gives another person the chance to grab the material before you or make a higher bid. The following tips will help you build a beautiful Tiny Home for a fraction of the cost.

Tip #1: Do All the Work Yourself

Okay, you might not be able to do all the work, but stretch yourself to do as much as you can. If you don't know anything about electricity and plumbing, you might need to seek professional help with that, but you would be amazed at what you can accomplish when you must. But when doing this ensure you're not using the time that you would normally make more money doing something your good at.

Essentially what I am saying is that if you work as an accountant or even a carpenter and you want to do the paining in your tiny home, don't take time off work to do this. Because think about it this way, if you are to make $400 a day at your normal job and you take 5 days off to paint your tiny home then you will be losing $2000 and if the tiny home could be painted in 3 days by a professional painter for $1500 then you will be losing 2 days of your time and $500. We want to be thinking and working smarter not harder!

Tip #2: Use Second-Hand Materials

Don't be surprised if you become the Craigslist king or queen as you build your Tiny Home. Look in the "for free" section on Craigslist first. Many people over-buy materials for home improvement projects, and they give the extra away if the buyer will just come and pick it up. You can find sinks, flooring, appliances, and a barrage of other things at no cost. With the popularity of renovation projects, it's a fertile field for finding used things that are still in great shape. The beauty of looking in the free section on Craigslist is that the products aren't always used, just left over from a large job. Leftovers from a larger build can be just enough to build your Tiny Home.

You can also become a frequent visitor at second-hand stores like Goodwill and Habitat for Humanity. Just because they don't have what you're looking for on the first visit, don't give up. They get different materials, furniture, and appliances in the store every day, so make these second-hand stores your favorites. The following is a list of what the owner of the above home got at Habitat for Humanity for a fraction of the cost.

- Windows (from $10 to $25)
- Exterior paint (five gallons for $20)
- Bathroom vanity ($8)
- Bathroom sink ($2.50)
- Ceiling fan ($20)
- Ceiling covering ($72)
- Roofing foam—insulated ($70)

There are also contractor stores where you can find new appliances, sinks, tubs, and timber that might have a small blemish and cannot be installed as new in a home. They sell these items quite inexpensively, but like everything else, you must be prepared to purchase on the spot. Some of the larger stores like Home Depot and Lowe's also have a section of culled timber where you can find framing timber for much less.

You can also look for flatbed trailers on Craigslist. This homeowner found a 14-foot trailer for only $800. Make sure you check it over carefully for any rust, corrosion, or damaged metal that could create an imbalance in the flooring of your Tiny Home. Another tip—find your windows first, then build your home to fit the windows you found. Windows are incredibly expensive, and you don't have to stick to any permits or codes, so you have the potential to design your room to fit the windows you find.

Trade and Barter

Don't be shy about asking someone to trade or barter. Perhaps you have something they could use and vice versa. Or, if you have a talent or skill that is popular, ask people if they are willing to make a trade. Let them know you're working on a tight budget to build a Tiny Home. Lots of people right now find Tiny Homes quite fascinating and will be more than willing to help.

Most of all, take pride in your accomplishment of building a Tiny Home for less than $10,000. Don't point out the flaws; instead, emphasize all the ways you saved money and still created something beautiful. You rock!

Building Your Tiny Home for $40,000 Plus

One of the following Tiny Homes will probably cost you $40,000 or more. You can see that instead of vinyl siding, they have used beautiful wood, and there's a deck around the Tiny Home. They have luxury items like oversized windows and French doors, as well as skylights. All these special features add to the cost of your Tiny Home. For many, these Tiny Homes would be a step-up home from their first build. Let's review what you could expect some of the costs to be on these types of Tiny Homes.

Estimated Costs for New Items and Materials

- Trailer ($5,000)
- Building plans ($1,000)
- Wood burning stove ($4,500)
- Skylights and windows ($4,000)
- Sheathing and lumber ($3,000)
- Siding ($3,000)
- Water heater ($1,200)
- Refrigerator ($900)
- Compost toilet ($1,500)
- Solar system ($3,000)
- Insulation ($1,500)
- Flooring ($500)
- Sinks, fixtures, tub, and shower ($2,000)
- Roofing ($1,000)
- Lighting ($700)
- Propane ($1,200)
- Countertops ($500)
- Front door ($500)
- Plumbing ($1,000)

These are all estimated prices, you can spend much more, and there are extra features and items to add to this price. These are just some of the initial expenses. If you don't plan on doing most of the work yourself, then you should also add construction costs to these figures. There's a broad range of costs for professionals, but a good rule of thumb is about $100 an hour.

Although you have your Tiny Home built, we haven't talked about where you're going to place it. Are you going to be mobile and leave it on wheels? Are you going to purchase or lease land and pour a slab on which to place your Tiny Home?

There are many variables, so it's difficult to determine what these costs would be. Are you going "off the grid" or do you plan to be hooked up to city services?

Hopefully, you have addressed these questions before beginning to build your Tiny Home. Whatever your plans are, building a Tiny Home should be challenging and fun. It should stretch you and make you proud of your accomplishments. Although building a Tiny Home will test you, it's a wonderful way to build more than a home—you'll also be building self-esteem and confidence. The best thing to do as you build is to create a plan and a budget and stick to it. Refuse to let others tell you it's impossible. If others can do it, so can you.

When you are facing some of the challenges in your build, just remember this is the first step to your new life. You are building a new future with your new Tiny Home, and there are bound to be some bumps along the way. With each hurdle you cross, you'll grow and create Tiny Home experiences and memories. So, as you struggle through some of the hardships of the build, keep your eyes on the prize and know that it will soon be worth it. You and your Tiny Home have a whole new life ahead of you, and you're accepting the challenge—the first of which is in the building.

It always helps to hear from others who have gone through what you are going through and come out the other side better for the experience. Take heart! You'll be hearing some of those success stories in the next chapter.

Chapter 8: Success Stories

The CNN Family Story

You might have heard of this family who was featured on CNN for their change in lifestyle to Tiny Home living. They are a family of four, have a large dog and a cat, and now live in a 168-square feet house. As you can see, they also make good use of their outdoor space and enjoy the outdoors a lot more than they used to when they lived in the city. They located their Tiny Home on land they had owned, so they are experiencing all the perks of a mortgage-free lifestyle.

Since May of 2011, they have spent a lot of time making their Tiny Home comfortable, and they both agree that it suits them perfectly. They have both reduced their work weeks to leave more time to go on bike rides, hikes, and work in the garden, and now spend more time with the kids. If they feel the need to get away from one another for a while, they'll take a nap or watch a movie in the loft and enjoy a bit of solitude.

An interesting thing that came out in the interview with CNN was that they discovered how distracting life had been by all the unnecessary things with which they had cluttered their lives. Now, they keep what they need and use it. It's just a whole new mindset and one that has enhanced their relationships with one another and their children.

Derek's Vermont Cabin

Derek had purchased land in the woods of Vermont in 2000, and he decided it was time to build a Tiny Home as a getaway for him and his family. Although it started much smaller, at just 200 square feet, his Tiny Home grew right along with those who wanted to share in Derek's weekend adventures. It is now 384 square feet of family fun. Derek built his Tiny Home himself, and it was a labor of love as he spent almost every weekend enjoying the outdoors and creating a wonderful Tiny Home that cost him next to nothing. Much of the materials were either donated, found curbside, or purchased at little Ma and Pa mills in Vermont where price haggling is considered an art form.

For example, Derek purchased his cedar roof rafters for only $40, and the wood for his staircase and deck cost a mere $50. Not only did he get his furniture free, as others tossed it aside, but he also found his windows curbside as well. When Derek looks over his accomplishments in building his Tiny Home, he takes pride in all his hard work, enjoys the discoveries he has made, and loves the extra time he gets to spend with family and friends. All in all, it's a lovely way to live.

Shirley's Place

It was a big decision for Shirley to move from Boston, and an even bigger one to decide to go tiny. The process of deciding what to keep and what to toss took almost as much time as building her Tiny Home, but after months of back and forth packing and discarding, she finally managed to pare it all down to living with only what she needs.

When Shirley moved her Tiny Home off the grid and into the country, she remembers how strange it first was not to hear the sounds of the city. Instead, she was hearing birds and watching nature rather than traffic. The projects in a Tiny Home are many, and Shirley is looking forward to her next one—building a wind turbine for power. Most of all, Shirley enjoys the pace of living in a Tiny Home. It's a worry-free lifestyle where you can take extra time enjoying a morning coffee without having to wait in line at Starbucks.

Ryan's Tiny Home

At 30-years-old, Ryan had been laid off from his job in a horrible economy. With the passing of each day, Ryan became more and more worried about how he was going to pay his bills. He had no savings with lots of debt, and the future was looking pretty bleak. That's when Ryan realized how much control everybody else had over his life. It was time to fight back, and Ryan did by building a Tiny Home.

Today Ryan has his own business, and it is independent of location, meaning he can move his Tiny Home anytime, anywhere. After 4 years of saving and building his Tiny Home one project at a time, Ryan now has the peace-of-mind that never again will anyone be able to take away his confidence and security.

Unsure of whether he would be able to live in a Tiny Home because of his larger size, Ryan faced the challenge head-on. His Tiny Home is 150 square feet, built on an 18-foot trailer.

He lives on a 32-acre parcel of land just a few minutes from town, but it seems like a world away from his other life.

Ryan loved his Tiny Home lifestyle so much that he now is the organizer of a Tiny Home Conference where other Tiny Home dwellers can gather and discuss how they overcame different challenges and new and inventive ways to conquer some of the issues of Tiny Home living. He is now enjoying a debt-free life and travels extensively, which was always a dream of his.

Ryan was not a contractor, plumber, electrician, and not even particularly handy with fixing things. He loves to show off his accomplishments and encourage others with his story, telling them that if he can do it with his limited resources and finances, they can do it even better.

Ryan didn't even own tools to build his Tiny Home and had to purchase them as needed. He had to make sure everything would fit his size, including furnishings, open living space, and a loft and stairs that were robust enough to support his weight. The results were beautiful, and the changes that Tiny Home living has made in his life is just as dramatic. Even though he lives a bit out of town, he has more friends now than ever, and he owes it all to Tiny Home living.

The advice Ryan has to give shows his fun-spirited sense of humor, as he tells other Tiny Home builders to make sure everything can fit through the front door and windows, including themselves.

Tiny Home Communities

Now that people realize that Tiny Homes is not a fad but a new way of life for the adventurous spirit, several builders are looking to create entire communities of Tiny Homes. It's like a village of small cottages, each one unique and reflective of the owner's personality. There's nothing "track" like about these homes; each street is filled with Tiny Home dwellers whose goal is to return to basics—to go back to a simple way of life. Keeping up with the Jones's is no longer about what you own, but about who you are. Don't we all have to return to this at one time or another? It's about building character instead of the biggest house.

The best success story will be your own as you begin the process of building your Tiny Home. Will you face challenges? Certainly! Will you overcome them and move forward a better person for the experience? Absolutely! There's nothing that will build character better than building a Tiny Home, and doing it with a family member allows you to create strong relationships along the way.

Whether you're building a Tiny Home for financial freedom, for a weekend getaway by the lake, or to live an eco-friendly lifestyle, the process will be enlightening. You'll learn the true measure of your worth, and it isn't in material things. Here are a few of the things you'll learn as you build and live in your Tiny Home.

- You learn to live simply, and you don't need the clutter around you that you've lived with all these years. No longer will you be moving box after box of junk from one house to another, when you can't even remember what they contain.
- You'll learn that you can do more than you ever dreamed possible. You can install cabinets, build steps, roof a house,

and build a deck. It's quite eye-opening to know how talented and self-sufficient you are.
- You'll learn to appreciate the simple things in life—a walk in the woods, swinging from a tree, or lounging on the deck in front of a fire.
- Your life will take on a different pace, and your relationships will have a genuineness to them that wasn't there in the past. You'll learn to listen to nature and hear her whispered appreciation of the steps you've taken to preserve her resources.
- Most of all, you'll feel a reward like no other. Instead of saying "I can't," your favorite phrase will be "I can do that."

Congratulations on your Tiny Home adventure! Enjoy every moment of its build and all the changes it will bring into your life.

Conclusion

Thank you again for taking the time to download this book!

Do you ever feel as though you're merely working to support your "things"—all the stuff you've gathered over the years and stored in your big house, but rarely use? Well, perhaps you are! If you long for a return to the simple life, then Tiny Home living might be just the ticket.

Don't miss out on this fantastic opportunity to build one, now that you have obtained the knowledge to do so.

You just need that little bit of money to start you're building works and you're set, so start saving and then you can invest in a nice ecofriendly affordable home.

If you enjoyed this book, please take the time to leave me a review on Amazon. I appreciate your honest feedback, and it really helps me to continue producing high quality books.

Other books written by Austin Knight:

Shipping Container Homes: The Perfect Guide to Building a Shipping Container Home for Sustainable Living, Including Plans, Tips, Cool Ideas, and More!

Interior Design: An Essential Guide On Home Decorating With Luxurious Style.

Lucid Dreaming: Lucid dreams: A Beginner's Guide On How To Control Your Dreams With Different Techniques

If you liked this book on a "Tiny house" go check out these other books above.

Made in the USA
Lexington, KY
18 February 2018